SCOTTISH
CASTLES

SCOTTISH CASTLES

*An Introduction
to the Castles of Scotland*

BY

the late W. DOUGLAS SIMPSON

C.B.E., M.A., D.LITT., LL.D., F.S.A., F.S.A. SCOT.
HON. F.R.I.A.S.

EDINBURGH
HER MAJESTY'S STATIONERY OFFICE
1959

© *Crown copyright* 1959

Published by
HER MAJESTY'S STATIONERY OFFICE

To be purchased from
13A Castle Street, Edinburgh EH2 3AR
49 High Holborn, London W.C.1
109 St. Mary Street, Cardiff CF1 1JW
Brazennose Street, Manchester M60 8AS
50 Fairfax Street, Bristol BS1 3DE
258 Broad Street, Birmingham 1
7 Linenhall Street, Belfast BT2 8AY
or through any bookseller

Price 5s. 6d. net

First published 1959
Fifth impression 1969

SBN 11 490168 6

CONTENTS

	Page
Foreword	ix
I. The Earliest Castles	1
II. Castles of Enceinte	6
III. The Early Tower Houses . . .	10
IV. Bastard Feudalism and the Later Castles	14
V. The Later Tower Houses . . .	17
VI. The Royal Palaces	19
VII. Firearms and the later "House of Fence"	20
VIII. The Scottish Baronial Style . .	21
Some Outstanding Scottish Castles . .	24
A Short List of Books and Papers . .	30

LIST OF ILLUSTRATIONS

PLATES

    I. Duffus Castle, Moray

   II. Cobbie Row's Castle, Orkney, interior of tower

  III. Kildrummy Castle, Aberdeenshire, from the air

  IV. Caerlaverock Castle, Dumfriesshire

   V. Affleck Castle, Angus

  VI. Borthwick Castle, Midlothian

 VII. Linlithgow Palace, West Lothian, palace and church from the air

VIII. Claypotts, Angus

  IX. Noltland Castle, Westray, Orkney

   X. Craigievar Castle, Aberdeenshire

  XI. Huntly Castle, Aberdeenshire

 XII. Earl's Palace, Kirkwall, Orkney

PLANS

1. Dinning Motte, Closeburn, Dumfriesshire (motte and bailey)
   Auldton Motte, Moffat, Dumfriesshire (motte and bailey)

2. Cobbie Row's Castle, Wyre, Orkney
   Castle Sween, Argyll

3. Kildrummy Castle, Aberdeenshire
   Caerlaverock Castle, Dumfriesshire

PLANS—*(continued)*

4. Bothwell Castle, Lanarkshire
5. Rothesay Castle, Bute
   Inverlochy Castle, Inverness-shire
   Loch Doon Castle, Ayrshire
6. Lochleven Castle, Kinross-shire
7. Threave Castle, Kirkcudbrightshire
8. Elphinstone Tower, East Lothian
9. Craigmillar Castle, Midlothian
   Affleck Castle, Angus
10. Tantallon Castle, East Lothian
11. Doune Castle, Perthshire
    Ravenscraig Castle, Fife
12. Borthwick Castle, Midlothian
    Greenknowe Tower, Berwickshire
13. Linlithgow Palace, West Lothian
14. Scalloway Castle, Shetland
    Claypotts, Angus
    Glenbuchat Castle, Aberdeenshire
15. Noltland Castle, Westray, Orkney
    Tolquhon Castle, Aberdeenshire
16. Earl's Palace, Kirkwall, Orkney

FOREWORD

THE Ancient Monuments Division of the Ministry of Public Building and Works now has under its charge a considerable and representative—though not as yet a complete—series of the ancient castles which form so characteristic a feature of the Scottish scene, and are associated with so much of interest in the historical, legendary, and literary lore of the country. Carefully preserved, so far as this is possible, against further decay, and, in most cases, surrounded by well-tended purlieus, these ruined castles yearly attract more and more interest, not only from the Scottish public but from the numerous English and overseas visitors who every summer throng to our noble northern land. At most of these castles, Official Guide Books are provided, which will help the visitor to realise that such a building is something more than a mere romantic ruin, that it has much to tell us about the social life of those who built and dwelt in it. It is for such serious students—and the number increases every year—that the present handbook has been written. Its aim is simply to give those interested a general conspectus of the origin and development of the Scottish castle, so as to enable them to fit each individual structure which they visit into its proper place in the sequence.

Those who read this little book will come to realise that, small and poor as it has always been, Scotland yet possesses a distinctive castellated architecture, and one of which any nation might be proud.

For the sake of completeness, reference has had to be made to a number of castles not in the Ministry's custody. All those which are looked after by the Ancient Monuments Division are distinguished by having their names printed in italics.

For an introduction to the subject generally, reference should be made to the corresponding English handbook in this series—*Castles*—written by the late Mr. Bryan H. St. John O'Neil, Chief Inspector of Ancient Monuments.

W. DOUGLAS SIMPSON.

King's College
Old Aberdeen
September 1958.

SCOTTISH CASTLES

I. *The Earliest Castles*

THE history of the Scottish castle begins in the twelfth century, when the powerful, far-seeing Kings of the Canmore dynasty began the process of integrating Scotland into the medieval state system of Western Europe, organising it as a strong feudal monarchy upon Anglo-Norman lines. Feudalism of the Norman pattern was a system by which ownership in land and responsibility for local government went hand in hand. Thus the castle of an Anglo-Norman landlord was much more than the gentleman's country house of modern times. In those unquiet ages it had of course to be a fortified country house; but it was more even than that, for it was also a centre of local government and military assembly. In his baron's court, the lord was empowered to deal justice among his tenants, alike in civil and criminal causes; and in the courtyard of the castle his tenantry gathered in arms when summoned to support him, either in his private quarrel or as the contingent due by him to the feudal army of the Crown, if he were a tenant in chief, or of his own superior if he were what was called a "mesne" tenant, holding his land from another baron greater in power than himself. In Scotland, from an early date, there was always a large number of small feudal tenants, and with the break up of the great ancient territorial lordships that followed the Wars of Independence their numbers increased even more. Each of these feudal lordlings, though he might hold no more than a few hundred acres, claimed the style of baron, and each had his fortified dwelling or castle. In England the fortification of squires' houses came to an end, broadly speaking, in the fifteenth century: but in the rowdy realm of Scotland every laird had to maintain a "house of fence" for nearly two centuries longer. It is due to these two causes—the great number of lairds and the long history of the "house of fence" in a disorderly land, that Scotland is today, *par excellence*, the land of castles. Here, if anywhere, we may say with truth that

> "Donjons, and towers, and castles grey
> Stand guardian by the winding way."

It is probably true that there are little less than 1000 castles of stone and lime still surviving, in whole or in part, throughout the length and breadth of the country; apart altogether from the remains of our earliest castles, which were made not of stone and lime but of timbered earthworks. Of the numbers of these latter castles, no census is available.

In Scotland there was no Norman conquest in the English sense. We should speak rather of a Norman penetration. Under the generous patronage of the Canmore kings, from David I onwards, large numbers of Anglo-Norman settlers migrated into Galloway, Lothian, the Central Lowlands and the north-eastern plains. Sometimes by Crown grants, at other times by marrying Celtic heiresses, they obtained extensive estates. Everywhere they introduced the feudal system, and its outward and visible symbol, the feudal castle —the private stronghold of a territorial magnate exercising devolved administrative and judicial authority over his tenantry. These castles were not the ponderous stone keeps of popular imagination. Even in England such costly structures were exceptional. The ordinary Norman castle was a thing not of stone and lime but of timbered earthwork—a moated mound crowned by a palisade enclosing a wooden tower. Often there was also a banked and palisaded courtyard sheltering the household buildings, likewise in wood. We may see pictures of these structures on the Bayeux Tapestry; and they were almost the only kind of castle that existed in Scotland during the Norman penetration in the twelfth century. The Norman name of them is a *motte*; where a courtyard is attached, it is known as the bailey, and the entire construction may be described as a *motte* and bailey or a mount and bailey castle.

In those parts of Scotland which were settled by Norman landholders or held by Celtic chiefs who had adopted the new system, remains of these earthwork castles are found (Fig. 1). One of the finest is *Duffus Castle*, near Elgin (Plate I). This was the original seat of the de Moravia or Moray family, now represented by the ducal houses of Atholl and Sutherland. The earthwork remains are most impressive, and are unique in Scotland by reason of the wide outer precinct ditch, enclosing eight acres, which surrounds the castle. This is not in any sense a military work, but corresponds to the wall which surrounds the "policies" of a modern country house. There is a similar precinct enclosure at Pleshy Castle, in Essex. In the fourteenth century the bailey was walled in, and a ponderous stone tower, of very fine workmanship, was erected on the mount, which has slipped under its weight, splitting the tower in two. Within the wall of the bailey are remains of a hall, reconstructed in the fifteenth century. It has been said that Duffus Castle rises from the Laich o' Moray "like a boss upon a buckler", and certainly it is one of the most impressive things of its kind in Scotland.

One of the noblest ruins in the guardianship of the Ministry is *Huntly Castle*, Aberdeenshire, the chief stronghold of the Gordons. Here the stately buildings erected by the "Cocks o' the North" stand amid the earthworks of a Norman *motte* and bailey castle on a grand scale, and the whole group of structures, in earthwork and in stone, presents an epitome of military construction from the twelfth to the seventeenth century. The story ends in earthwork as it began; for the latest addition to the defences, still well preserved, is a ravelin of the Civil War period.

At *Castle Urquhart* on the shores of Loch Ness, Inverness-shire, we have a large stone castle also constructed upon the earthworks of a mount-and-bailey. Here, as at Windsor Castle, there has been a double bailey. The *motte* occupies the site of a vitrified fort, dating from the prehistoric Iron Age.

Parallel to the introduction of the Anglo-Norman baronage with their earthwork castles came the Anglo-Norman clergy bringing the Roman discipline and organisation, as they had developed on the soil of the old Empire during the centuries when Celtic Scotland was largely isolated from the European states-system. Gradually the country was divided up into parishes, each served by a parochial priest, and the parishes were grouped into dioceses, each presided over by a bishop. So alongside the feudal castle two new items, the parish church and the cathedral, were added to the Scottish scene. In many cases the parish was just the manor of a feudal baron, ecclesiastically considered, and the parish church began as the private chapel of the lord of the manor. That is why to this day in Scotland the remains of a Norman castle are so often found close beside the parish church. Church and castle, side by side, represent respectively the ecclesiastical and the civil nuclei of the early parochial organisation.

From the outset in England there existed, alongside the earthwork castles, a number of castles built in stone and lime. These were of course expensive structures, and, as a rule, could be afforded only by the kings or the greater barons. Typically, such castles took the form of a great square tower —the Norman "keep" of writers from the sixteenth century onwards, though the older term for them was *donjon*, or simply "the great tower". The most famous of all these Norman keeps is, of course, the *Tower of London*. It was founded by William the Conqueror, and therefore belongs to the eleventh century. So do the keep of Colchester Castle and one or two others: but the great building period of these stone keeps in England was in the twelfth century.

In Scotland, it was for long denied that any stone castles existed during the period of the Norman penetration. This is most unlikely, as the Normans were great builders in masonry, and it seems absurd to suppose that the noble patrons who founded such fine Norman cathedrals and abbeys as Kirkwall, Kelso or Dunfermline, or rich parish

THE EARLIEST CASTLES

churches like Leuchars and Dalmeny, were not equally able to employ the same masons to house themselves in castles of stone. At *Edinburgh Castle* the rich little Norman chapel of St. Margaret still remains, and it can hardly be imagined that the powerful kings of the House of Canmore who erected it were incapable of building a stone tower and curtain on the castle rock. The Wars of Independence bore hard on our early stone castles, most of which were destroyed by the Scots themselves on their recapture from the Southron. Moreover, in the more central parts of the country early stone castles, even if they escaped destruction in the wars, tended to be rebuilt or replaced by structures of a newer fashion. It is in the remoter parts of the country, unaffected by the English wars and less influenced by changes in fashion, that we should expect to find the most ancient stone castles in Scotland.

In point of fact, the oldest datable Scottish castle of stone is in a part of the country which, when it was built, did not belong to Scotland at all. Until 1468 the northern islands belonged to Norway; and the *Orkneyinga Saga* tells us how about 1145 a Norse chief, Kolbein Hruga, built a fine stone castle (*steinkastala*) in *Wyre*, a small island in the Orkneys. Here there still survives the stump of a small rectangular tower, enclosed in a circular ditch, and associated with later buildings (Fig. 2, Plate II). The name of the founder, in a corrupted form—"*Cobbie Row's Castle*"—is still attached to the ruin: and close beside it is the twelfth century chapel of St. Mary, now in ruins. Excavation failed to yield traces of any earlier structure on the site of the present castle, and there can be little doubt that the existing remains represent the *steinkastala*. In their own country, the Norsemen of the twelfth century were well up to building stone castles, as the recent excavations at King Sverre's, near Trondheim have shown. And in Orkney itself, the stately Norman Cathedral of St. Magnus teaches us that the Norse Jarls of the Northern Isles were able to command the services of masons of the highest status, drawn from the great centres of ecclesiastical architecture: for it is clear, on stylistic grounds, that the master mason who designed Kirkwall Cathedral was brought hither from Durham.

Another twelfth century castle survives in an outlying part of Scotland, likewise under Norse control at the time of its construction. At *Castle Sween*, in Knapdale, Argyllshire, we find what appears to be, typologically considered, the earliest stone castle in Scotland (Fig. 2). It is said to have been built by Dougall, third chief of Craignish, early in the thirteenth century, and the main structure presents the appearance of a gutted Norman keep, with large pilaster and angle buttresses. The round-arched doorway, placed in one of these pilasters, reminds one of the so called "Jew's House" in Lincoln. A great oblong tower-house, with pointed loop-holes, and a cylindrical angle tower, are later additions. This castle was destroyed by Colkitto Macdonald in 1645.

II. Castles of Enceinte

During the thirteenth century—the "Golden Age" of Alexander II and III—stone castles began to be common in Scotland. The finest castles of this prosperous era, such as *Dirleton*, *Kildrummy* (Fig. 3, Plate III), *Bothwell* (Fig. 4), and *Caerlaverock* (Fig. 3, Plate IV), are beautifully built of dressed ashlar, and have large round towers flanking curtain walls enclosing a courtyard. The walls and towers together are known as the *enceinte*: usually one tower is larger than the others, and forms the keep or *donjon*. Generally this tower is placed at the remotest corner of the *enceinte*. Within the latter are the domestic buildings—hall, kitchen, "solar" or lord's suite, chapel and so forth—and these also are, as a rule, placed on the side of the courtyard furthest from the entrance—always the point of danger in a castle.

Probably the finest of our thirteenth century castles of *enceinte* has been *Bothwell*—though the original scheme

PLATE I. *Duffus Castle*

PLATE II. *Cobbie Row's Castle: interior of tower*

(Reproduced by permission of Skyviews and General Ltd., Leeds 11)

PLATE III. *Kildrummy Castle, from the air*

PLATE IV. *Caerlaverock Castle*

PLATE V. *Affleck Castle*

PLATE VI. *Borthwick Castle*

PLATE VII. *Linlithgow Palace and St. Michael's Church, from the air*

(from a photograph in the Cambridge University collection of air photographs)

PLATE VIII. *Claypotts*

PLATE IX. *Noltland Castle*

(Country Life photo)

PLATE X. *Craigievar Castle*

PLATE XI. *Huntly Castle*
Renaissance Fireplace in Upper Hall

PLATE XII. *Earl's Palace, Kirkwall*

appears never to have been completed, and one half of its great donjon was thrown into the Clyde when the castle was dismantled by the Scots in 1336. This splendid tower, beautifully built of fine polished ashlar, with rich Gothic detail, is isolated from the castle courtyard by its own proper moat. In this respect it recalls the now destroyed French Chateau de Coucy. At *Kildrummy Castle* the internal arrangements of the donjon closely recalled those of Coucy; and it cannot be without significance that Alexander II, in whose reign *Kildrummy Castle* was founded, married, in 1239, Marie de Coucy, the daughter of the builder of the great French chateau. *Kildrummy* is perhaps the most complete example of an elaborately constructed thirteenth century castle of *enceinte*. Its curtain walls, with four round towers, in greater or less preservation, the hall and the chapel with its three-light Gothic window, belong in substance to the original fabric. The great gatehouse is an addition of Edward I's time, and there is evidence that it was erected by the famous Savoyard architect, James of St. George, who designed Edward's great castles in North Wales, such as *Conway*, *Caernarvon*, and *Harlech*. *Kildrummy*—justly hailed as the "noblest of northern castles"—was the ancient seat of the Earls of Mar. It played a memorable part in Scottish history from the Wars of Independence until the "Fifteen", when it was dismantled.

The shell of another fine thirteenth century castle remains at *Rothesay* in Bute (Fig. 5), the cradle of the Royal Stewarts. Here the *enceinte* is circular, with four round towers, and both walls and towers are faced with fine ashlar. In this castle we have preserved the original parapet, with its battlements, all sealed up, like a fossil, as it were, in a subsequent heightening of the wall. The great forework is an addition of the sixteenth century, and we shall have to consider it later in its own context. Inside the courtyard, the only feature that now bulks large is the chapel, which also is of late date. In 1230 *Rothesay Castle* stood a notable siege by the Norsemen, who hewed their way through the wall with axes, "for the stone was soft". The east curtain shows signs of much disturbance and partial rebuilding, and here, no doubt, the Norwegians made their breach.

On the western seaboard of Scotland—a region remote (as we saw) from the causes of destruction or rebuilding—we find an interesting and well preserved group of thirteenth century castles of *enceinte*, not all yet in the custody of the Ministry of Public Building and Works. This group of castles represents the advent of the power of the feudal monarchy on the threshold of the Hebrides, prior to the conquest of these after the victory at Largs in 1263. The most famous, and most accessible of these, is *Dunstaffnage*, near Oban in Argyllshire. Here the walls of *enceinte* and round towers are all in good preservation. The architectural detail points to a mid-thirteenth century date, and close beside the castle is the ruined chapel, one of the loveliest gems of First Pointed Gothic in all Scotland. At Inverlochy Castle, Fort William, Inverness-shire (Fig. 5), we have a simple massive quadrangular *enceinte* with round towers, one of which forms the donjon. In the other castles of this western group, Mingary, on the Point of Ardnamurchan, Argyllshire, and Castle Tioram, on an island in Loch Moidart, Inverness-shire, the nature of the rocky site did not permit of towers, and so we have the *enceinte* castle in its simplest form, consisting of a plain multangular curtain wall. The same primitive form, but associated with the finest ashlar masonry and Gothic detail, is to be found in the island castle of *Loch Doon* (Fig. 5), which stood a famous siege in 1335. When the water level in Loch Doon was raised to serve a hydro-electric scheme, this beautiful ashlar work, perhaps the finest secular masonry of the thirteenth or early fourteenth century in Scotland, was transported by the Ministry of Public Building and Works, stone by stone, and re-erected on the mainland.

A great rubble-built curtain wall of the thirteenth century forms the oldest part of *Balvenie Castle*, Dufftown, Banffshire. This was the ancient castle of Mortlach, a stronghold of the Comyns, visited by Edward I in 1303. Outside the wall is a

CASTLES OF ENCEINTE

most impressive rock-cut ditch. The masonry of this curtain wall closely resembles that of another famous Comyn castle, Lochindorb in Badenoch, Inverness-shire—later the chief stronghold of the "Wolf of Badenoch". This castle dates from about the end of the thirteenth century and illustrates the omission at this time of the *donjon* or keep. The purely passive idea of defence embodied in the *donjon* theme began now to give way to a more active, aggressive conception centred on the gatehouse, which tended to become the most important defensive feature of the castle, forming a complete self-contained residence for the lord or castellan, who thus had the weakest point in the castle under his direct control. Structures of this kind may therefore be described as "keep-gatehouses". The Edwardian gatehouse at *Kildrummy* already mentioned, was of this type, and another such is known to have been built by Master James of St. George at *Linlithgow* in 1304. The remains of a third still survive, embodied in a later tower-house, at the royal castle of *Dundonald* in Ayrshire.

Another feature characteristic of the late thirteenth century is the tendency to reduce the courtyard area, until this finally becomes a mere close girt around by a cluster of towers—the whole now forming the *donjon* or lord's residence, and being usually associated with an outer court and quarters for the general household. This clustered *donjon* type is well illustrated at *Dirleton* in East Lothian, where the thirteenth century remains are again characterised by the fine quality of the ashlar masonry.

Before leaving the subject of our stone castles dating from before or during the struggle for independence, notice must be taken of two examples which were never of the *enceinte* plan. At *Hailes* in East Lothian, we have what is not so much a castle as a fortified manor house, which as originally built must have resembled the well known Aydon Castle in Northumberland. Significantly, *Hailes* was built by the Gourlay family, who held much land in Northumberland. And at Yester in the same shire, on a mount-and-bailey site, a stone *donjon* with a "marvellous *souterrain*, wonderfully constructed" is known to have been erected by the lord of the manor, Hugh Gifford, who died in 1267. This *souterrain*, with its massive ribbed vault, beautifully built of ashlar work, still remains, and is one of the finest pieces of secular architecture, dating from before the War of Independence, which survives in Scotland. On one side a ribbed and vaulted passage conducts down to a well, and on the other a similar passage leads to a postern gate opening in the steep bank upon which the castle is built.

III. The Early Tower Houses

In Scotland the first half of the fourteenth century was taken up with the two long and desolating Wars of Independence. It is a time of which the chroniclers tell us far more about the casting down of castles than about their building up. Not until the end of the century did the country begin to recover from the devastating effects of the long wars. Comparatively few castles were built during this unhappy period: and these for the most part take the form of simple rectangular tower-houses—reverting in principle to the old Norman keep. The typical medieval house consisted of a central hall, with kitchen and offices at its lower end, and the owner's private rooms at the upper. Sir Walter Scott has given us a vivid picture of this type of house in his description of Rotherwood, Cedric the Saxon's dwelling in *Ivanhoe*. Where defensive considerations have controlled the plan, the rooms, instead of being extended horizontally, are piled on top of one another, so as to form a tower-house—exemplified in the same novel by Front-de-Boeuf's Norman keep of Torquilstone. The tower-house is thus nothing else than a specialised form of the normal medieval hall-house, up-ended for reasons of security. In Scotland, with its long-continued history of unsettlement, foreign and domestic war, the tower-houses found especial favour as the simplest and cheapest form in which a landowner, be he a great baron or a small laird, could provide himself with a dwelling at once strong in itself, suitable to his domestic needs, and with its brow-beating height flaunting his social pride. No other country in the world has rung the changes more thoroughly on the tower-house theme. Successively modified to suit improved domestic standards and altered conditions of defence, the Scottish tower-houses, by their ingenuity of design and effectiveness of aspect, represent a distinctive and valuable contribution to the general achievement of medieval architecture.

Three of the finest of our fourteenth century tower-houses are *Lochleven Castle*, Kinross-shire (Fig. 6), *Dundonald Castle*, Ayrshire, and *Threave Castle*, Kirkcudbrightshire (Fig. 7). *Lochleven Castle* stood a notable siege in 1335, but the existing tower-house dates from later in the century. It contains five storeys, and the entrance, reached only by a ladder, is on the second floor. Such tower-houses usually had appended to them a courtyard enclosed by a curtain wall—all, however, on a much smaller scale than the great thirteenth century *enceintes*. The Scottish name for such an appended courtyard is a *barmkin*. At *Lochleven* the barmkin wall is well preserved, with a round tower added in the sixteenth century. A small part of the barmkin wall may be a remnant of the castle besieged by the English in 1335. *Lochleven Castle* is famous all the world over as the scene of the imprisonment of Mary Queen of Scots, in 1567.

The royal castle of *Dundonald* contains a very large rectangular tower-house, which is of particular interest as it embodies the stump of an Edwardian keep-gatehouse. The reconstruction can be identified by heraldic and other evidence as the work of Robert II, the first Stewart King (1371–90). The barmkin wall survives, and the whole structure stands impressively on a hill top, girt by the ramparts of a prehistoric *dun*.

The great tower of *Threave Castle* was built towards the end of the fourteenth century by Archibald the Grim, third Earl of Douglas and Lord of Galloway. It is perhaps the most impressive thing of its kind in Scotland, and gains enormously in effect by its site on an island in the River Dee. Here also the barmkin wall is well-preserved. It is known to have been constructed in the panic that followed the disaster of Flodden.

One of the earliest of these tower-houses in Scotland forms the oldest portion of Drum Castle, Aberdeenshire, since 1323 the seat of the Irvine family. The tower was the chief place of the old royal forest of Drum, and there are details which suggest that it may have been already in existence by the year 1300. In Aberdeenshire also is the similar but now ruined tower of Hallforest, the hunting seat of the royal forest of Kintore. David II was here on more than one occasion.

A house consisting of four storeys of single rooms, one on top of the other, reached by a ladder to a door on an upper floor, and for internal communication possessing but a single spiral stair, may be strong, but is not convenient. Very soon, therefore, we find the Scottish builders endeavouring to provide a certain degree of family privacy by hollowing out their massive walls into a series of mural closets. The greater the degree to which this practice was carried out, the later will be the tower-house. In the fifteenth century, the wall, which externally presents an appearance of plain massive strength, may thus come to conceal a perfect labyrinth of mural stairs and closets. The two finest examples of this peculiarity are Comlongon Castle, Lord Mansfield's seat in Dumfriesshire, and the Tower of Elphinstone in Midlothian (Fig. 8). In some of the larger towers of this century, the architectural detail, such as enriched fireplaces, aumbries or wall-presses, and such like, can be very fine. A good example is *Cardoness Castle* in Kirkcudbrightshire.

The Scottish master-masons were not long content with their endeavour to provide private accommodation by hollowing out wall chambers within the mass of their rectangular towers. Before the end of the fourteenth century they hit on the idea of building the tower with a wing—*Scoticè*, a *jam*—appended to a long side of the main building. Thus we have what may be called the L-plan. This plan gave a lot of what was chiefly wanted, namely, private accommodation, since the rooms in the wing did not need to be as high as the lofty halls in the main structure, and therefore there could be five or six storeys of private rooms in the *jam* corresponding to the three or four storeys in the main portion. Not only that, but the new plan also provided a very strong position for the doorway, in the "re-entrant angle", as it is called—tucked in, so to speak, between the projecting limbs of the building. Hence in these L-towers the doorway is commonly brought down to ground level—another gain in comfort.

One of the finest fourteenth century L-towers forms the kernel of the famous Castle of *Craigmillar* near Edinburgh (Fig. 9). Another, of about the same date, is at Dunnottar Castle in the Mearns. Much ingenuity is displayed in the plans of such tower-houses. That maxim of all good planning, that "the container should be equal to the contained"—the required accommodation being achieved without waste space and without overcrowding or awkwardness—was thoroughly understood by our old-time Scottish architects. One of the most masterly examples of such planning in an L-tower, on quite a small scale, can be studied at *Affleck Castle*, in Angus, near Dundee (Fig. 9, Plate V).

In all such towers—as indeed generally in the medieval castle, whatever its plan—defence was conducted mainly from the wall-head. This was crowned by a "crenellated" parapet—i.e., the wall was broken up into alternate voids and solids, *embrasures* from which the archer shot, and *merlons* behind which he sheltered while re-loading his crossbow. It is a simple parapet of this kind which is sealed up in later work at *Rothesay Castle* (see p. 7). Another fine early parapet of the same time remains unaltered on the tower of Drum. In time of war, extra command of the ground at the foot of the castle was sometimes provided by oversailing timber hoardings. The putlog holes for such a war-head may still be seen at *Rothesay*. In the fifteenth century, it became customary to crown the castle with a stone oversailing corbelled parapet, a *machicolation* or open space being left between each pair or corbels, though which missiles or heated liquids could be cast down upon the assailants. These fifteenth century machicolated parapets provide a most effective feature in some of our Scottish towers, for example at Comlongon. At *Craigmillar Castle* a curtain wall with angle towers, all machicolated in this way, was drawn round the tower-house early in the fifteenth century. Fine machicolated towers form a prominent feature in the fifteenth century reconstructions of *Bothwell Castle*, Lanarkshire, and of *Caerlaverock Castle*, Dumfriesshire. *St. Machar's Cathedral* in Aberdeen has its twin western towers fortified in this way.

IV. Bastard Feudalism and the later Castles

It is a mistake to imagine a medieval castle as constantly manned by an alert garrison, armed to the teeth. When the lord was in residence it would contain his *familia* or household, doubtless including, in a large establishment, a few men-at-arms. In his absence there might be no one else than a caretaker. Should war approach the castle walls, the garrison would be provided from the lord's feudal tenantry, called up for the purpose. In some of the greater castles, a tenant might hold his land by "castle-guard", being bound to provide the garrison, say for a particular tower. At *Dover Castle*, for instance, some of the towers still retain the names of the tenants so charged with their defence. Under the feudal system, a tenant was normally required to provide not more than forty days' military service each year. Short-term, untrained levies of this sort became increasingly inadequate to sustain the great conflicts of the later Middle Ages, such as the Wars of Scottish Independence and the Hundred Years War in France. War, in fact, was now becoming a scientific business, for which a professional, highly-trained soldiery was required. Hence everywhere in the later Middle Ages the kings and the greater barons betook themselves to the practice of commuting the military service due by their tenants for monetary payments, or payments in kind that could be converted into money; and with the ready cash thus available they hired professional soldiers. It was largely with such soldiers that Edward III and Henry V conducted their campaigns in France. At home, it was with private armies so enlisted that the overmighty barons of England fought each other to death in the Wars of the Roses, and their Scottish contemporaries kept their country in chronic uproar by their incessant feuds among themselves, and their struggles to obtain control of the feeble monarchs of the Stewart House. To this new kind of feudalism of the later Middle Ages—an illegitimate offspring (as it were) of the genuine article—the name of Bastard Feudalism has been applied.

Upon the castle plan, bastard feudalism exercised a profound influence. Quarters had now to be found for a standing mercenary garrison; and these *lanzknechts* were apt to be awkward and indeed sometimes dangerous neighbours, lacking the natural fidelity of the feudal tenant to his overlord. Two things therefore were necessary. Barrack quarters must be found for the mercenaries; and the lord must provide himself with a self-contained residence for his own person and his *familia*, having the entrance to the castle under his personal control.

In the Edwardian keep-gatehouses we have already noted the beginnings of this development. It was arrested in Scotland by the troubles of the fourteenth century, during which, as we saw, not many new castles on a large scale were built. But the end of that century saw the erection of one or two major castles which illustrate very clearly the impact of bastard feudalism on castellar construction. Earliest of these —in existence by the year 1374—is the mighty castle of the Douglases at *Tantallon*, in East Lothian (Fig. 10). Its principal feature is the vast curtain wall, spanning the promontory from cliff to cliff, and resting at either end on a powerful cylindrical tower. In the middle is the gatehouse, which serves also as a residence, well appointed and well secured, for the lord or castellan. Inside the castle are not one but two great halls, one above the other. The lower of these is fitted up as a mess room for the garrison, the upper is a festal hall of the traditional pattern. One of the grandest ruins in Scotland, *Tantallon Castle* is famous not only in the sober page of history but also in the romantic verse of Scott's *Marmion*.

A little later than *Tantallon* is Doune Castle in Menteith, Perthshire (Fig. 11), the great stronghold of the all-powerful Dukes of Albany, built in the closing years of the fourteenth century. Here, in striking contrast to such an earlier castle as *Kildrummy*, the weight and mass of the structure are no longer reserved, but are brought forward and concentrated on the front line. Upon this, all the principal buildings are deployed: behind, the castle tails off into a mere screen wall, and there is no "great tower" or *donjon*, isolated in a corner like those of *Bothwell* and *Kildrummy*. Instead, we have in the forefront of the castle a complete, self-contained structure, forming a separate habitation for the lord or governor, and including the well secured entrance, which is thus under the lord's personal control. This composite structure—gatehouse and lord's residence in combination—is quite separate from a suite of domestic buildings, hall, kitchen, and the rest, also forming part of the frontal mass, yet having no communication with the lord's residence, and obviously apportioned to the general body of the garrison or retainers.

With this splendid castle we reach the highest achievement of perfected castellar design in Scotland. In this respect, it strongly recalls the contemporary Chateau de Pierrefonds in France.

The great forework added by James IV and James V to the ancient *enceinte* of *Rothesay Castle* illustrates the same theme. It combines a strongly planned gatehouse with a fine suite of royal apartments.

One of the most interesting of the later Scottish castles is *Ravenscraig* in Fife (Fig. 11). This was built by James II as part of a scheme of coastal defence: and in the *Exchequer Rolls* the building accounts are in part preserved. Work was begun in 1460, but the building was left uncompleted at the King's death three years later. *Ravenscraig* is of great interest, because it was apparently the first castle in Britain to be designed for systematic defence by cannon.

V. *The Later Tower-Houses*

Apart from such large and exceptional structures as *Tantallon*, Doune, and *Ravenscraig*, the majority of the castles built in later medieval Scotland were designed upon the traditional tower-house plan. Whether of the simple rectangular pattern, or built with a *jam* on the L-plan, these Scottish towers display an almost inexhaustible variety of design, and strikingly reveal the resource and pliancy of their architects. Some of the largest, like the great rectangular tower added in the fifteenth century to the palace of the Bishops of Moray at Spynie, near Elgin, or the massive L-tower of *Auchindoun Castle*, Banffshire, built by the master-mason, Thomas Cochran, the ill-starred favourite of James III, reach the scale of a good-sized Norman keep.

At *Edzell Castle*, Angus, the stronghold of the Lindsays of Glenesk, we have a fine L-tower of the early sixteenth century. Here the *jam* is devoted to the spiral staircase. Contemporary with the tower at *Edzell*, and resembling it in some of its architectural features, though differing in design, is the remarkable tower which forms the kernel of *Craignethan Castle*, Lanarkshire—the Tillietudlem of Scott's *Old Mortality*.

By far the finest Scottish tower-house is Borthwick Castle in Midlothian (Fig. 12, Plate VI). The licence to build it was granted in 1430. This majestic castle is executed with a beauty of masonry and richness of design unsurpassed in any like structure in the British Isles. It is entirely built of stone, vaulted in all its height, and the stone-slabbed roof rests directly on the uppermost vaults. The weight of this tower has been computed at not less than 20,000 tons; of this, 12,000 tons are accounted for by the ashlar work with which all the surfaces, inside and out, are cased. The splendid machicolated parapet, with its angle turrets, lends a most imposing aspect to the building. Borthwick Castle is remarkable in that it has not one but two *jams*, both on the same side, so that the plan comes to resemble the letter E, with the middle bar struck out. On the main floor, the central building contains the great hall: at its lower end is the kitchen in one of the *jams*, while the "solar" or lord's room opening from the dais end of the hall, occupies the other. Thus with great skill, advantage is taken of its elaborate plan to recover, in a tower-house, the normal horizontal disposition of the medieval hall-house plan. Borthwick Castle, which is still inhabited, was besieged by Cromwell in 1650. "If you necessitate me to bend my cannon against you," tersely wrote the Lord Protector, "you may expect what I doubt you will not be pleased with." The result is seen today in a great gash which disfigures the ashlar masonry on the east front.

The numerous tower-houses on the L-plan built up and down the country for the lairds, or smaller barons, during the sixteenth century present a subject of inexhaustible charm and interest. The flexibility shown in their planning is truly remarkable. A favourable example is *Greenknowe Tower* in Berwickshire (Fig. 12), dated 1581. Here the *jam* is occupied by the main stair as far as the first floor, but above this it contains private rooms, and both these and the upper rooms of the main house are served by a turret stair in the re-entrant angle. This tower still retains its iron *yett*, the bars of which have their mode of intersection reversed in opposite quarters, a mode of construction peculiar to Scotland.

VI. The Royal Palaces

It was in the sixteenth and seventeenth centuries, under the later Stewarts, that the royal palaces—*Edinburgh Castle, Holyroodhouse, Stirling Castle, Linlithgow Palace* (Fig. 13, Plate VII), and Falkland Palace, assumed their present form. In these buildings, as might be expected, we find evidence, both documentary and in the fabric, for the employment of French craftsmen. At *Edinburgh Castle*, the great hall, with its hammer-beam roof, dates from the early sixteenth century. At *Stirling*, Cochran's Hall, built by the unlucky favourite of James III, has been, perhaps, the finest thing of its kind in Scotland; while the royal apartments, erected by French masons, are an early and quaint example of Renaissance architecture. The only medieval portion still surviving at *Holyroodhouse* is the tower built by James IV. It much resembles the gatehouse tower at Falkland Palace. In the ruined east wing of the latter building we can again study the handiwork of French sculptors. The *Palace of Linlithgow* remains, roofless indeed, but otherwise intact, as the finest example of late medieval planning in Scotland. Although the existing fabric dates from several building periods extending between the fourteenth and the seventeenth centuries, it displays surprising uniformity in design. Its situation, overlooking the loch, remains in all its unspoiled beauty, and the great fifteenth century town's kirk, which closely adjoins it, combines with the Palace to form a group of medieval architecture unsurpassed in Scotland.

VII. Firearms and the Later "House of Fence"

In *Ravenscraig Castle*, 1460–3, we have seen a fortalice systematically designed for defence by "falconets" or small cannon. Cannon, however, were a prerogative of the Crown, and it was not until hand-guns came into general use during the sixteenth century that provision for firearms began to be introduced in the "houses of fence". The effect upon their plan was immediate and striking. Hitherto, as we saw, defence for a tower-house was mainly from its war-head—i.e., it was conducted in a vertical plane: and so our old Scottish towers are, in general, tall and narrow of aspect. But now, when the possibility of flanking defence by hand-guns at ground level became apparent the problem of defence revolved through a quadrant, from the vertical to the horizontal plane. Immediately the castle plan begins to undergo a lateral expansion, as the opportunities are realised of defending the main structure by *jams* or wings no longer set out at right angles but diagonally, or *en échelon* to use the military phrase. Thus the old L-plan is replaced by a tower-house with a wing set out diagonally at one corner, so as to command, with gunloops, two sides of the main building. Blairfindy Castle, Banffshire, and *Scalloway Castle* in Shetland (Fig. 14) are examples of this plan, which may be described as a "two-stepped" castle. From this stage, the next development was obvious: to build the "house of fence" with not one, but two, flanking towers, echeloned at diagonally opposite corners. Each tower covers two faces of the main structure, and the latter in its turn covers the towers, so that it is impossible to approach such a castle from any quarter whatever without coming under fire. Not only this, but the flanking towers provided a great deal of private accommodation, at a time when, with improved social standards, this was increasingly in demand; and the *jams* being set diagonally to the main house did not interfere so much with its lighting as if they had been built out straight from one face. Thus the "three-stepped" or Z-plan became a very favourite one in Scotland, and upwards of sixty examples are known, mostly in the North East. A remarkable example, near Dundee, is *Claypotts*, Angus (Fig. 14, Plate VIII). It bears the dates 1569 and 1588. Here the two towers are round, but are corbelled out to the square above in a remarkably picturesque manner. The ground floor is well provided with wide mouthed gunloops, *Glenbuchat Castle*, Aberdeenshire (Fig. 14), dated 1590, is a fine example with square towers. Here the stair turrets are supported, not on the usual corbelling, but by *trompes* or squinch arches in the French manner. *Muness Castle* in Unst, Shetland—the most northerly castle in Britain—is a Z-building, dated 1598, with round towers. But the most remarkable of our Z-castles is *Noltland* in Westray, an island of the Orkneys (Fig. 15, Plate IX). Here the towers are square, and the walls all round are pierced with tiers of gunloops, giving the castle the semblance of some ancient man o' war's hull. No other British castle exhibits provision for firearm defence on anything like such a scale. The picturesque castle of *Tolquhon*, in Aberdeenshire (Fig. 15), built (except for the "Auld Tour") between 1584 and 1589, is an interesting example of the Z-plan applied to a courtyard castle.

VIII. *The Scottish Baronial Style*

Scottish castellated architecture reaches its climax about the turn of the sixteenth and seventeenth centuries. Much of the landed property of the ancient church had fallen into the hands of the lairds, and their new-found wealth expressed itself in an outburst of building. More settled internal conditions, and the end of wars with England after the Union of the Crowns, were also circumstances favourable to fine architecture. So the ornate castellated mansions of this latest period such as Glamis, Fyvie, Castle Fraser, Midmar and Craigievar (Plate X), with their regal coronets of pointed turrets and crow-stepped gables and their riotous profusion of corbelling, form a group of buildings of which any nation might be proud. Although these castles are often described as of French origin, they are in fact purely native in plan and style, and the master-masons, where their names are on record, are always Scotsmen.

It was not until this late period that Scotland as a whole began to respond to the influence of the Renaissance. Now at last, neo-classical motives began to appear on dormer windows, finials, and such like external details, and in the plaster work and other interior decoration. Painted ceilings now became common: the Ministry of Public Building and Works has good examples in its charge at *Huntingtower*, Perthshire, *Culross Palace*, Fife, and *Kinneil House*, West Lothian. Nithsdale's building in *Caerlaverock Castle*, dating from 1638, is a pure and exquisite specimen of the early Classical Renaissance. Foreign masons were now employed by some of the greater barons, as well as by the kings. At *Crichton Castle*, Midlothian, we have a diamonded Italianate façade, obviously inspired by the *Palazzo dei Diamanti* at Verona, and the Italian connection is supported by the builder, Earl Bothwell's known association with that country. The great row of oriel windows at *Huntly Castle*, Aberdeenshire, recalls those at Blois, and it is known that a French mason worked for the first Marquis of Huntly, who reconstructed his castle between 1600 and 1604 (Plate XI). And at *Edzell Castle*, Angus, we have a unique decorated garden wall, dated 1604, with sculptured representations of the Cardinal Virtues, the Liberal Arts, and the Planetary deities. These are of German origin, and their presence here is explained by ascertained facts in the history of the builder, Lord Edzell.

Of all the castellated buildings belonging to this latest period in old Scottish secular architecture, by far the most accomplished is the *Earl's Palace* at Kirkwall, in the Orkneys (Fig. 16, Plate XII). The great array of oriel and bay windows shows that the master mason had a scholarly acquaintance with French architecture: nevertheless the detail is purely native, and there is no reason to doubt that the architect was a Scotsman.

The blight of Calvinism, and the outbreak of the long and cruel wars of religion, nipped in the bud this tender blossom of the Scottish Renaissance, and put an end, for a full generation, to the art of fine building. After the Restoration in 1660, more settled conditions returned, but the old generation of master masons had died out, and the way was thereby opened for the pure Classical Renaissance, exemplified in such stately palaces as Drumlanrig Castle, Dumfriesshire, Kinross House, Kinross-shire, and the main portion of the Palace of *Holyroodhouse*. In the houses of the country lairds, however, and in the burghs, the old building traditions survived, more and more feebly, until as late as the eighteenth century. Among the town houses of the lairds, the finest are *Argyll's Lodging*, Stirling, the *Palace of Culross*, Fife, and Provost Skene's House in Aberdeen, recently well restored by the city corporation.

SOME OUTSTANDING SCOTTISH CASTLES

Only one important part of the structure of a castle is necessarily relevant to the group in which it is included (sometimes a castle of several periods is included in more than one group). Castles italicised are under the care of the Ministry of Public Building and Works and are normally open to visitors daily. Many of the others are scheduled Ancient Monuments; others yet are still inhabited.

The intending visitor to Ancient Monuments should consult the *Illustrated Guide to Ancient Monuments, vol. VI, Scotland* (see Book-List, p.30).

Mottes and Motte and Bailey Castles (page 2)

Aberdeenshire	*Huntly Castle*
	Doune of Invernochty, Strathdon
	Bass of Inverurie
	Peel of Lumphanan
	Tillydrone, Motte-Hill
Argyll	Achadunan Motte, near Lochgilphead
Dumfriesshire	Auldton Motte, Moffat
	Barntalloch Motte, Langholm
	Motte of Dinning, Closeburn
	Tinwald Motte
	Wamphray Motte
Fife	Maiden Castle, Windygates, Markinch
Inverness-shire	*Urquhart Castle*
Kirkcudbrightshire	Balmaclellan Motte
	Boreland Motte, near Kirkcudbright
	Dalry Motte
	Ingleston Motte, near New Abbey

SOME OUTSTANDING SCOTTISH CASTLES

Kirkcudbrightshire	Motte of Urr
Lanarkshire	Carnwath Motte
	Coulter, Motte Hill
Moray	*Duffus Castle*
Roxburghshire	Hawick Motte
Wigtownshire	Ardwell Motte
	Droughdool Motte, near Dunragit
	Druchtag Motte, Mochrum
	High Dunmore Motte, Kirkmaiden

Stone castles of the 12th or early 13th century (page 5)

Argyll	*Castle Sween*, Knapdale
Caithness	*Castle of Old Wick*
Orkney	*Cobbie Row's Castle*, Isle of Wyre

Castles of Enceinte, mostly 13th century (page 6)

Aberdeenshire	*Kildrummy Castle*
Argyll	*Dunstaffnage Castle*, near Oban
	Mingary Castle, Ardnamurchan
Ayrshire	*Loch Doon Castle*
Banffshire	*Balvenie Castle*, Dufftown
Bute	*Rothesay Castle*
Dumfriesshire	Auchencastle, near Beattock
	Caerlaverock Castle
	Tibbers Castle, near Carronbridge
East Lothian	*Dirleton Castle*
Inverness-shire	Castle-Tioram, Loch Moidart
	Inverlochy Castle, Fort William
	Kisimul Castle, Barra
	Roy Castle, Nethybridge
Kincardineshire	Kincardine Castle
Lanarkshire	*Bothwell Castle*
Moray	Lochindorb Castle
Perthshire	Kinclaven Castle

Gatehouse Castles (page 9)

Aberdeenshire	*Kildrummy Castle*
Ayrshire	*Dundonald Castle*
Bute	*Rothesay Castle*
Dumfriesshire	*Caerlaverock Castle*
	Lochmaben Castle
East Lothian	*Tantallon Castle*
Perthshire	Doune Castle

Tower-Houses of late 13th and 14th century (page 10)

RECTANGULAR

Aberdeenshire	Drum Castle
	Hallforest Tower
Ayrshire	*Dundonald Castle*
Clackmannanshire	Alloa Tower
Dumfriesshire	Torthorwald Castle
Fife	*Aberdour Castle*
Kinross-shire	*Lochleven Castle*
Kirkcudbrightshire	*Threave Castle*, near Castle Douglas
Moray	*Duffus Castle*

L-PLAN

Kincardineshire	Dunnottar Castle
Midlothian	*Craigmillar Castle*

15th century Tower-Houses (page 17)

RECTANGULAR

Angus	*Broughty Castle*
Argyll	*Kilchurn Castle*, near Dalmally
Ayrshire	Mauchline Castle
Clackmannanshire	*Castle Campbell*, Dollar
	Sauchie Tower, Alloa
Dumfriesshire	Comlongon Castle
	Gilnockie Tower (Hollows Tower)
East Lothian	Elphinstone Tower, Tranent

SOME OUTSTANDING SCOTTISH CASTLES

Fife	Balgonie Castle
Kinross-shire	*Burleigh Castle*
Kirkcudbrightshire	*Cardoness Castle*
Lanarkshire	Mains Castle, near East Kilbride
Moray	Spynie Palace
Selkirkshire	Newark Castle, Philiphaugh
Stirlingshire	Bardowie Castle

L-PLAN

Angus	Inverquharity Castle, Kirriemuir
Banffshire	*Auchindoun Castle*, Glenfiddich
Peeblesshire	Neidpath Castle
Roxburghshire	Cessford Castle
West Lothian	Niddrie Castle, Kirkliston

OTHER PLANS

Midlothian	Borthwick Castle
Roxburghshire	*Hermitage Castle*

Later (16th–17th century) Tower Houses (page 18)

RECTANGULAR

Aberdeenshire	*Corgarff Castle*
Argyll	Saddell Castle, Kintyre
Dumfriesshire	Amisfield Tower
	Repentance Tower, Hoddam Bridge
	Spedlin's Tower, near Templand
Lanarkshire	*Craignethan Castle*
Moray	Coxton Tower
Perthshire	Aldie Castle
Roxburghshire	*Smailholm Tower*
Selkirkshire	Kirkhope Tower
West Lothian	Midhope Tower
Wigtownshire	Craigcaffie Tower

L-PLAN

Aberdeenshire	Craigievar Castle
	Delgaty Castle, Turriff
	Leslie Castle, Kennethmont

Angus	*Affleck Castle*, Monikie
	Braikie Castle, Inverkeilor
	Edzell Castle
	Glamis Castle
Argyll	Barcaldine Castle
Ayrshire	Maybole Castle
Banffshire	Blairfindy Castle
	Fordyce Castle
Bute	*Lochranza Castle*, Arran
Fife	*Scotstarvit Tower*, Ceres
Kincardineshire	Crathes Castle
	Fiddes Castle
Kirkcudbrightshire	*Carsluith Castle*
	Drumcoltran Tower
Midlothian	Merchiston Castle, Edinburgh
Perthshire	Pitheavlis Castle, Perth
Selkirkshire	Oakwood Tower
Wigtownshire	*Castle of Park*, Glenluce
	Dunskey Castle, near Portpatrick
Zetland	*Scalloway Castle*

Z-PLAN

Aberdeenshire	*Glenbuchat Castle*
	Midmar Castle
Angus	*Claypotts*
Ayrshire	Kelburn Castle
Fife	Fordell Castle
Orkney	*Noltland Castle*, Isle of Westray
Ross and Cromarty	Ballone Castle

ROUND

Kirkcudbrightshire	*Orchardton Tower*

OTHER PLANS

Aberdeenshire	Barra Castle
Angus	Kellie Castle, Arbroath
Argyll	Dunderave Castle
Ayrshire	Killochan Castle

East Lothian	Luffness House
Fife	Kellie Castle
Roxburghshire	Darnick Tower

Other outstanding late castles and domestic buildings (pages 19-22)

Aberdeenshire	Provost Ross's House
	Provost Skene's House
	Tolquhon Castle
Angus	Melgund Castle
Argyll	*Carnasserie Castle*, Kilmartin
Ayrshire	Auchans House
	Rowallan Castle
Banffshire	Boyne Castle, Portsoy
Caithness	Girnigoe Castle and Castle Sinclair, Wick
East Lothian	Northfield House, Preston
Fife	*Culross Palace*
Kinross-shire	Tullibole Castle
Kirkcudbrightshire	*Maclellan's Castle*, Kirkcudbright
Lanarkshire	*Craignethan Castle*
Orkney	Earl's Palace, Birsay
	Earl's Palace, Kirkwall
Peeblesshire	Drochil Castle
	Traquair House
Perthshire	*Elcho Castle*
	Huntingtower
Renfrewshire	*Newark Castle*, Port Glasgow
Roxburghshire	Ferniehirst Castle
	Queen Mary's House, Jedburgh
Stirlingshire	*Argyll's Lodging*, Stirling
Aberdeenshire	*Huntly Castle*
Angus	*Edzell Castle*
Dumfriesshire	*Caerlaverock Castle*
Midlothian	*Crichton Castle*
Stirlingshire	*Stirling Castle*
	Mar's Wark, Stirling

A SHORT LIST OF BOOKS AND PAPERS

D. MacGibbon and T. Ross, *Castellated and Domestic Architecture of Scotland*, 5 volumes 1887-1892. The *Inventories* of the Royal Commission on Ancient and Historical Monuments, Scotland (*Berwickshire; Caithness; Dumfriesshire; East Lothian; Edinburgh, City of; Fife, Kinross and Clackmannan; Galloway; Wigtownshire and Kirkcudbrightshire; Midlothian and West Lothian; Orkney and Shetland; Outer Hebrides, Skye and the Small Isles; Peeblesshire; Roxburghshire; Selkirkshire; Stirlingshire; Sutherland;* are published).

S. H. Cruden, *The Scottish Castle*, 1960; W. Mackay Mackenzie, *The Medieval Castle in Scotland*, 1927; G. Scott-Moncrieff, *The Stones of Scotland*, 1938; W. Douglas Simpson, *Exploring Castles*, 1958. There are many papers on individual castles and aspects of their history in *Proceedings of the Society of Antiquaries of Scotland* (indexed to 1947); also *Antiquaries' Journal* (Loch-an-Eilan Castle, 1937; Bastard Feudalism, 1946), *Archaeological Journal* (Abergeldie, 1954), *Trans. Ayrshire Archaeo. and Nat. Hist. Soc.* (Dundonald Castle, 1947-9), *Trans. Glasgow Archaeo. Soc.* (Rothesay Castle, 1937; Breachacha Castle, 1939; Castle Tioram and Mingary Castle, 1954).

PLANS

In order to shew the relative size of comparable monuments, the plans are reproduced at two uniform scales. The first, 1:1200, is used for earthworks and for the larger castles. Smaller castles and tower-houses are reproduced at twice this scale, 1:600.

The dates on the plans refer to the works shewn in solid black, to which particular reference is made in the text.

FIGURE I

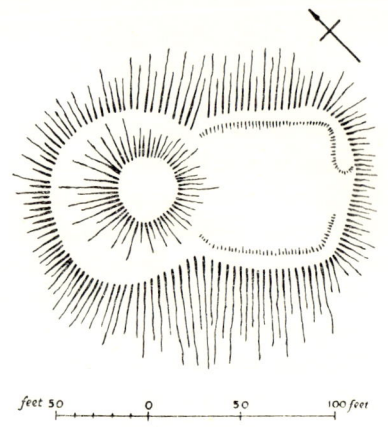

Dinning Motte

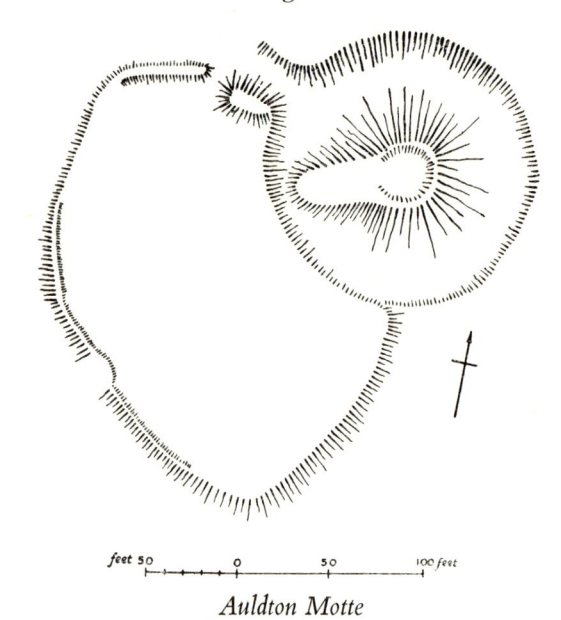

Auldton Motte

FIGURE 2

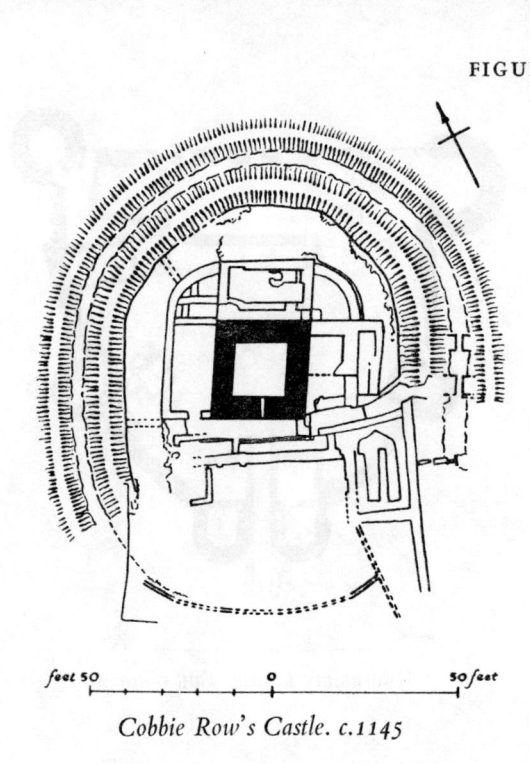

Cobbie Row's Castle. c.1145

Castle Sween. 12th century

FIGURE 3

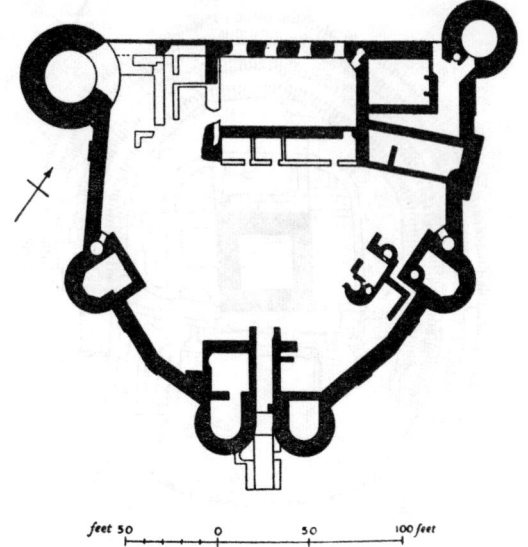

Kildrummy Castle. 13th century

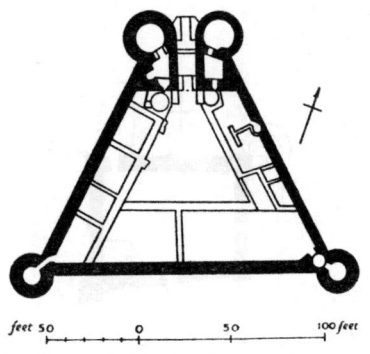

Caerlaverock Castle. Late 13th century

FIGURE 4

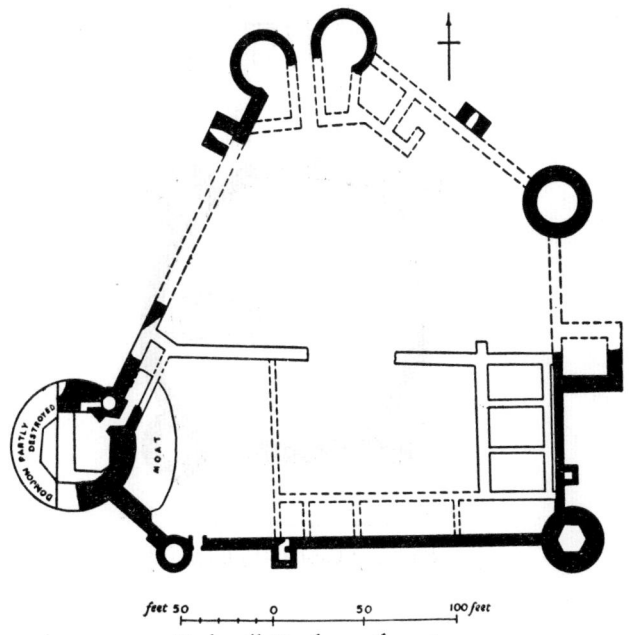

Bothwell Castle. 13th century

FIGURE 5

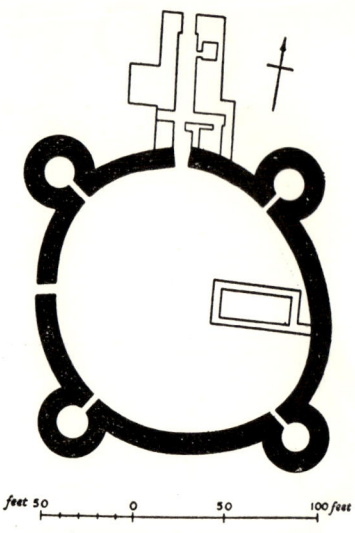

Rothesay Castle. 13th century

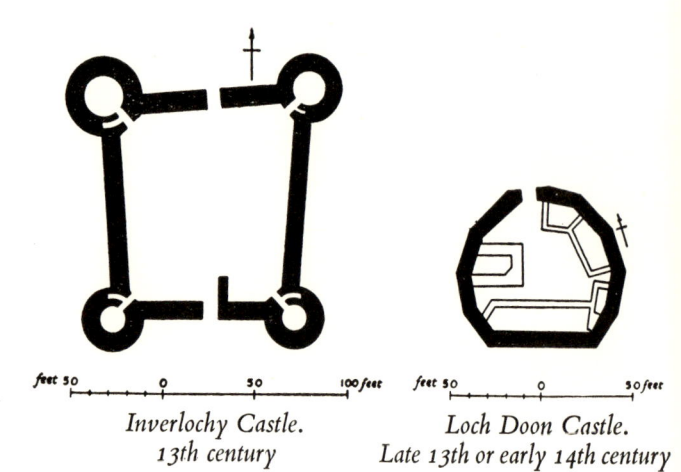

Inverlochy Castle.
13th century

Loch Doon Castle.
Late 13th or early 14th century

FIGURE 6

INTERMEDIATE FLOOR

SECOND FLOOR

GROUND FLOOR

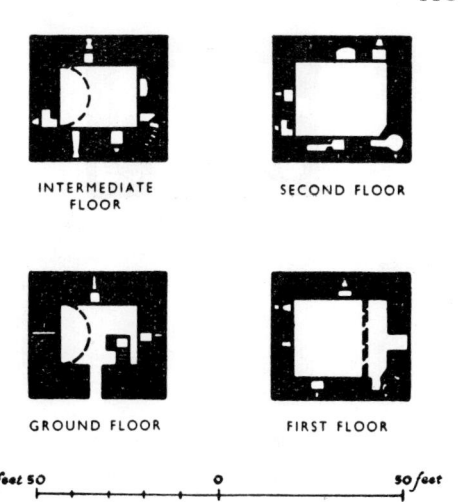

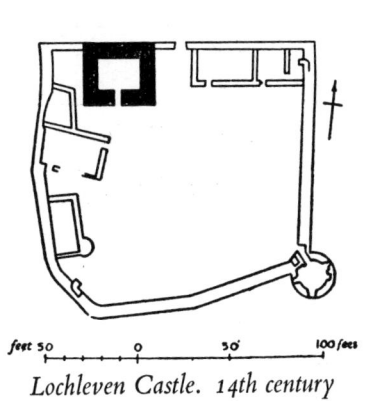

FIRST FLOOR

feet 50   0   50 *feet*

feet 50   0   50'   100 *feet*

Lochleven Castle. 14th century

FIGURE 7

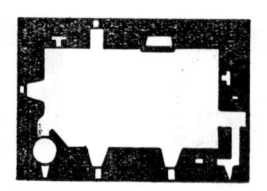

FIRST FLOOR

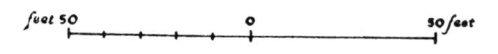

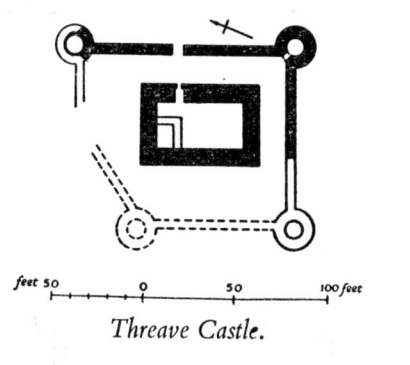

Threave Castle.

Tower, 14th century

FIGURE 8

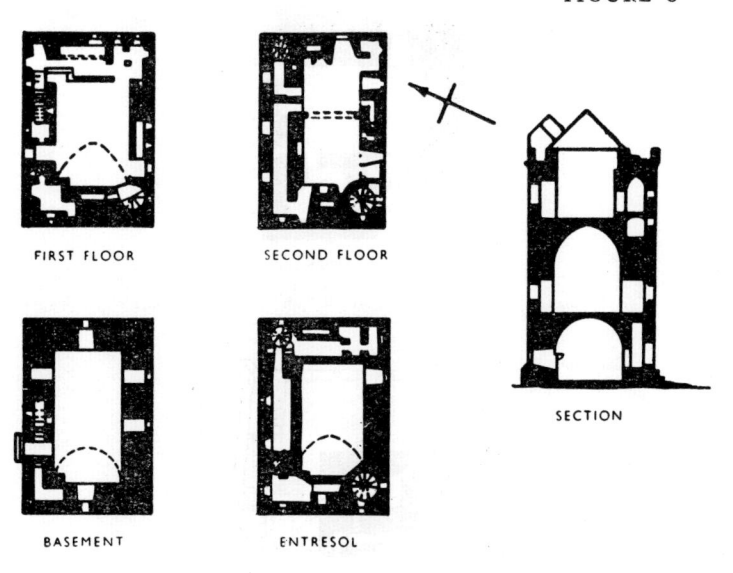

FIRST FLOOR

SECOND FLOOR

BASEMENT

ENTRESOL

SECTION

feet 50   0   50 feet

Elphinstone Tower. 15th century

FIGURE 9

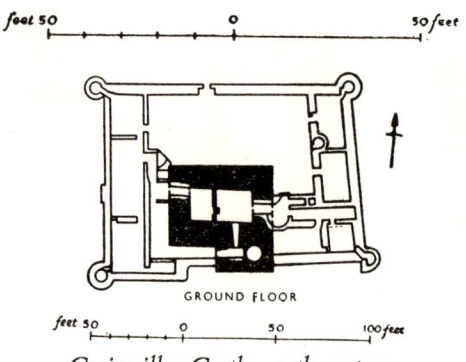

FIRST FLOOR

GROUND FLOOR

Craigmillar Castle. 14th century

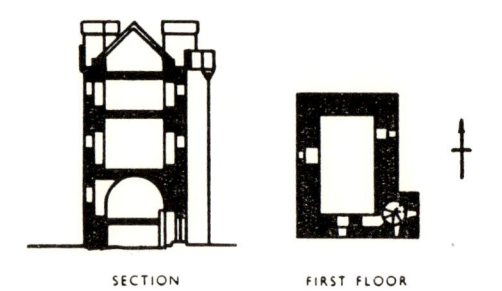

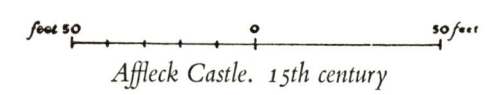

SECTION   FIRST FLOOR

Affleck Castle. 15th century

FIGURE 10

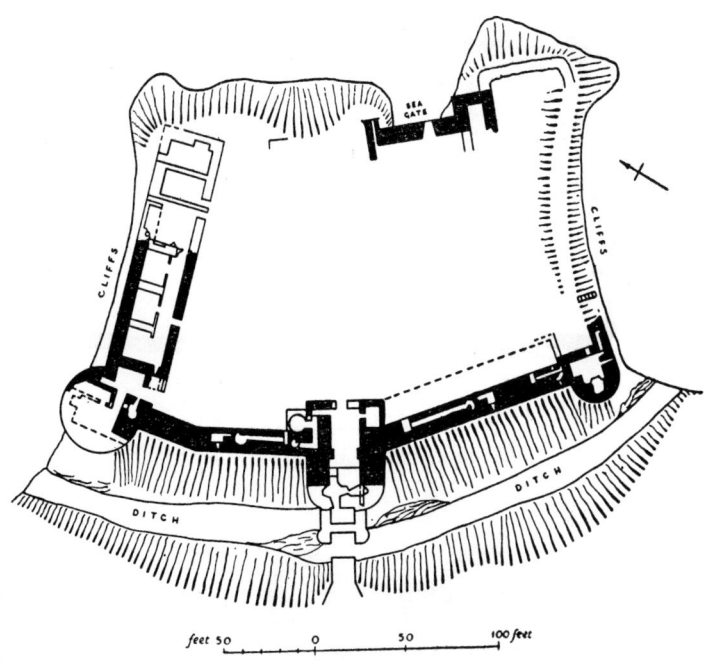

Tantallon Castle. 14th century

FIGURE 11

BASEMENT　　　　　　　　　　　FIRST FLOOR

feet 50　　0　　50　　100 feet

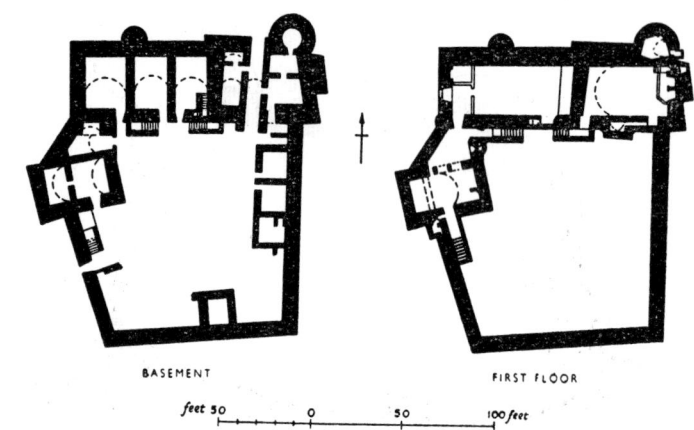

Doune Castle. Late 14th century

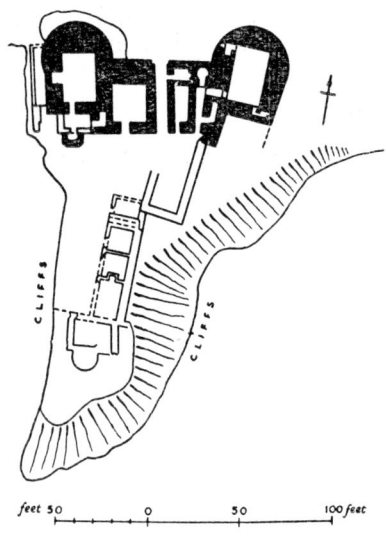

feet 50　　0　　50　　100 feet

Ravenscraig Castle. Begun 1460

FIGURE 12

*Tower-house after 1430;
outer wall and tower later*

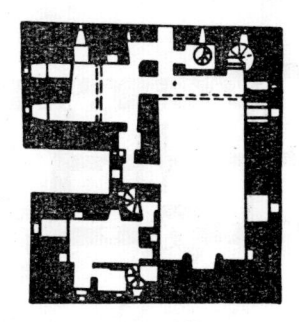

FIRST FLOOR

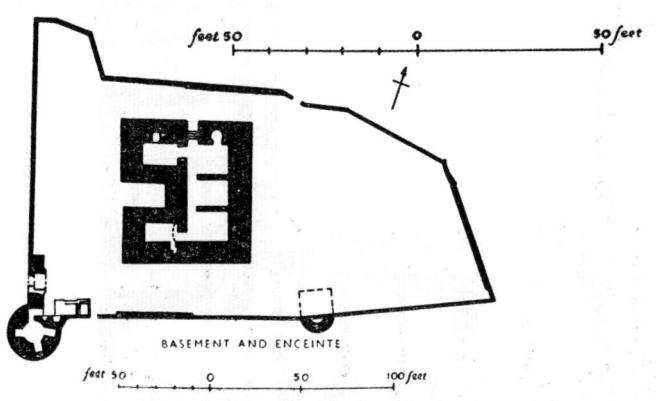

BASEMENT AND ENCEINTE

Borthwick Castle

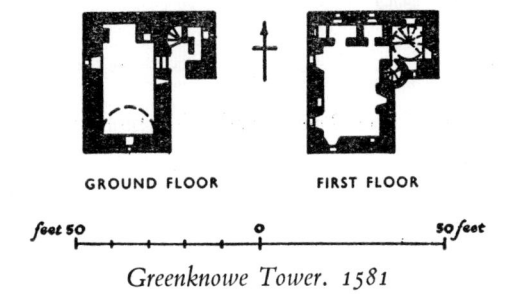

GROUND FLOOR   FIRST FLOOR

Greenknowe Tower. 1581

FIGURE 13

feet 50   0   50 *feet*

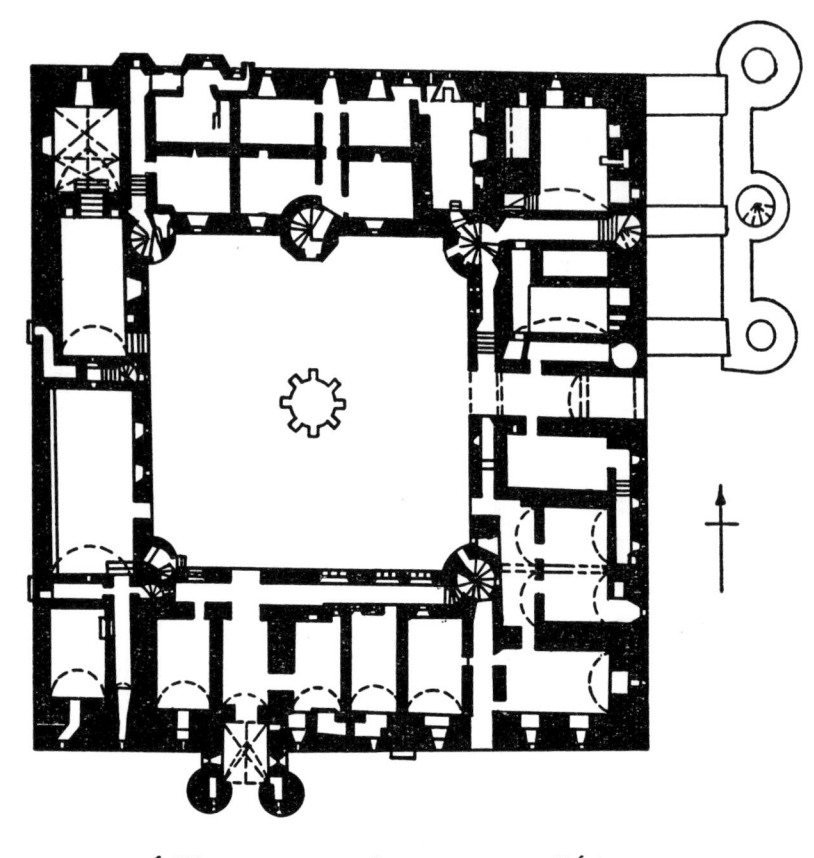

Linlithgow Palace. 15th-17th centuries

FIGURE 14

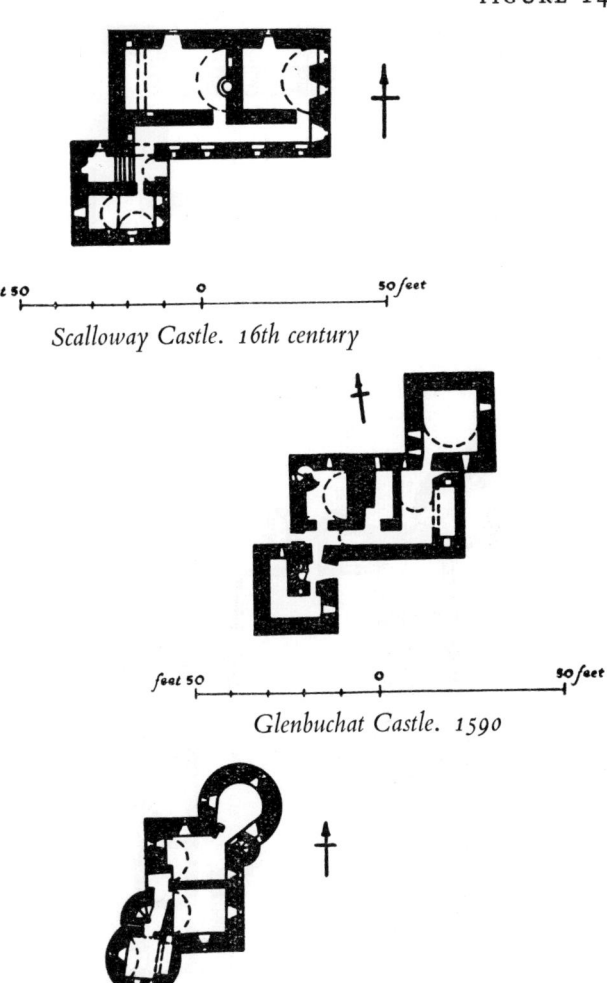

Scalloway Castle. 16th century

Glenbuchat Castle. 1590

Claypotts. 1569-88

FIGURE 15

feet 50   0   50 *feet*

Noltland Castle. 16th century

feet 50   0   50 *feet*

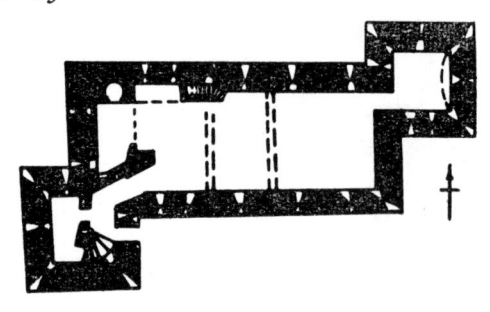

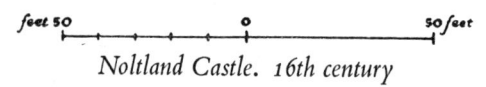

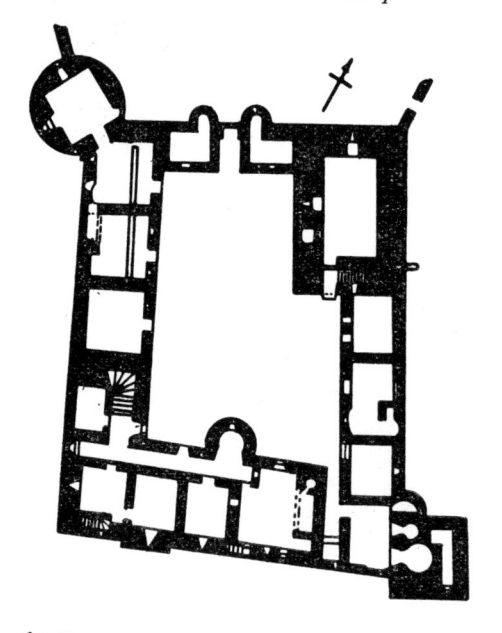

Tolquhon Castle. 1584-89 save for N.W. Tower

FIGURE 16

FIRST FLOOR

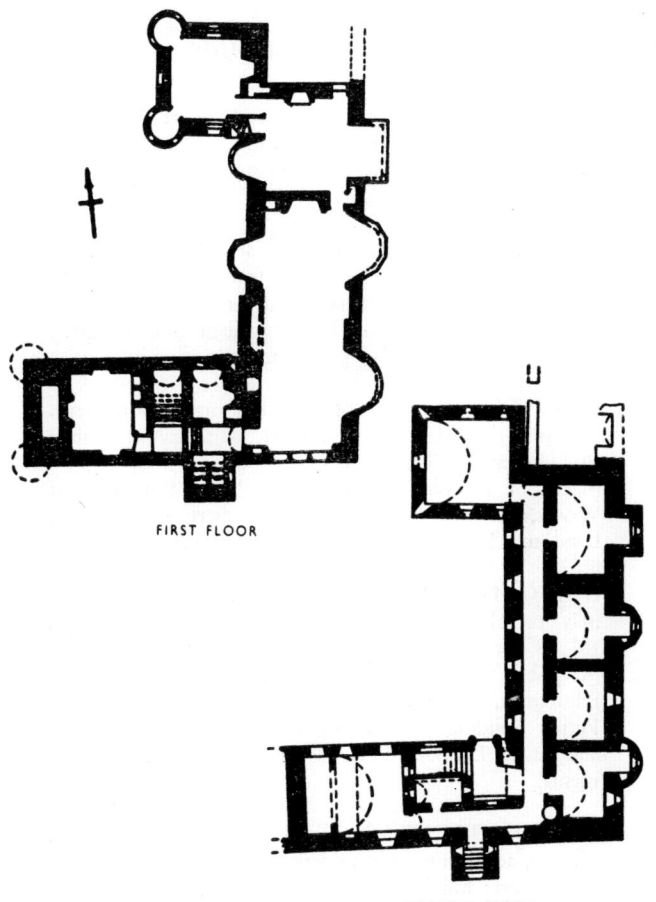

GROUND FLOOR

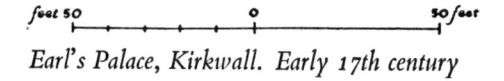

Earl's Palace, Kirkwall. Early 17th century

Ancient Monuments and Historic Buildings

Many interesting ancient sites and buildings are maintained as national monuments by the Ministry of Public Building and Works. Guide-books, postcards and specially produced photographs are available as follows:

GUIDE-BOOKS or pamphlets are on sale at most monuments and are also obtainable from the bookshops of H.M. Stationery Office. A complete list of titles and prices is contained in Sectional List No. 27 available free on request from any of the addresses given on cover page iv.

POSTCARDS can be purchased at many monuments or from the Clerk of Stationery, Ministry of Public Building and Works, 122 George Street, Edinburgh, 2 (Clerk of Stationery, Ministry of Public Building and Works, Lafone House, 11-13 Leathermarket Street, London, S.E.1 for English and Welsh monuments).

OFFICIAL PHOTOGRAPHS of most monuments may be obtained in large prints (e.g., size $8\frac{1}{2}'' \times 6\frac{1}{2}''$; $10'' \times 8''$) at commercial rates from the Librarian, Ministry of Public Building and Works, Broomhouse Drive, Edinburgh, 11 (Photographic Librarian, Ministry of Public Building and Works, Hannibal House, Elephant and Castle, London, S.E.1, for English and Welsh monuments).

SEASON TICKETS, valid for 12 months from date of issue, admitting their holders to all ancient monuments and historic buildings in the care of the Ministry, may be obtained from the Ministry or at many monuments.

Printed in Scotland by Her Majesty's Stationery Office Press, Edinburgh

Dd. 239008 K120 2/69 (5775)